Sarah McCann.

D1356734

The Abbreviated PSALTER
of the Venerable BEDE

The *Abbreviated* PSALTER
of the *Venerable* BEDE

Translated by

GERALD M. BROWNE

William B. Eerdmans Publishing Company

Grand Rapids, Michigan / Cambridge, U.K.

WM. B. EERDMANS PUBLISHING CO.
255 Jefferson Avenue SE, Grand Rapids, Michigan 49503 /
PO Box 163, Cambridge CB3 9PU UK

www.eerdmans.com

Printed in the United States of America

06 05 04 03 02   7 6 5 4 3 2 1

Library of Congress Cataloging-in-Publication Data

Collectio psalterii Bedae Venerabili adscripta. English
    The abbreviated psalter of the Venerable Bede /
translated by Gerald M. Browne.
        p.   cm.
    ISBN 0-8028-3919-3 (cloth : alk. paper)
    1. Psalters.   I. Bede, the Venerable, Saint, 673 – 735.
    II. Browne, Gerald M.   III. Title.

    BX2033.A4 B7613   2002
    264′.028 — dc21

                                2001040533

Design by Kevin van der Leek, Praxis, Vancouver.
This book has been composed in FF Quadraat.

The photographs on pp. 26, 34, 42, 50, 58, 66, 74, 82, and 90 are from W. Arndt,
Schrifttafeln zur Erlernung der lateinischen Palaeographie II, ed. 2 (Berlin, 1888), plate 42,
a facsimile of a ninth-century manuscript page of Bede's *Abbreviated Psalter*.

Except for the cathedral at Durham and the remnants of Hadrian's wall, the northern parts of Northumberland in England are a bit off the normal tourist's path, and its post-industrial wasteland seems to have little to offer apart from urban sprawl. But there, tucked away in a tiny corner of the otherwise unremarkable town of Jarrow, stands the Royal Ancient and Monastic Parish Church of St. Paul, a part of which dates back to over 1300 years.

After entering the church, the visitor will soon come upon the Foundation Stone, whose Latin text reads in translation: "The Dedication of the Church of St. Paul on April 23rd in the fifteenth year of King Ecgfrith and the fourth year of Ceolfrith, the Abbot and under God's guidance the founder of the same church."

The year in question is A.D. 685, but at that time dating in B.C. and A.D. was not yet in common use. Things, however, were soon to change, for amongst the first inhabitants of the Benedictine monastic community centered around the church lived the priest Bede, whom posterity has surnamed the Venerable. Born in 672 or 673, Bede is best known today for his *Ecclesiastical History of the English People*, which — though written in Latin — is justly regarded as the first important work of English literature. It was in that work that Bede, as he traced the development of the church in England, made popular the method of dating events before and after the birth of Christ.

Bede was also the author of biblical commentaries, didactic treatises, saints' lives, sermons and religious poems. The most eminent scholar of his age, he practiced the Benedictine principle of stability and never ventured far from Jarrow, where he died peacefully in 735. His tomb may now been seen in the Galilee Chapel of Durham Cathedral.

At the end of the *History* Bede sums up his life: "I was born in the territory of this monastery," and "at the age of seven was entrusted for my education ... to the most reverend Abbot Benedict and then to Ceolfrith [named in the Foundation Stone quoted above]. Since then I have spent the entirety of my life in the same monastery, devoting all my effort to the study of the scriptures. And amidst the observance of the duties of the Rule and the daily task of chanting in church, I have always found delight in learning, teaching and writing."

What Bede says about his "observance of the duties of the Rule and the daily task of chanting in church" requires our attention, for here he provides insight into the *Abbreviated Psalter*.

The Rule (*Regula* in Latin) of the Benedictine monastery to which Bede belonged offered the monk a complete guide to life. It centered around the *Opus Dei*, "the Work of God," an elaborate liturgy focusing on the Psalter (i.e., the Book of Psalms) and requiring that it be chanted in church in its entirety every week. As a Benedictine monk, Bede devoted eight hours every day of his life to reciting the Psalter in accordance with the strictures of the *Opus Dei*. His day began around 2:00 A.M. for the first service in the church, and it continued — with interruptions for work and study — until about 6:30 P.M.

Although we do not know precisely which Rule Bede's monastery followed, it is likely to have been very close to the well-known Rule of St. Benedict. The reader may like to see the selection of Psalms which that Rule required for Sunday, arranged in accordance with the hours of service (Psalms repeated every day are in boldface).

Vigils (Matins):	**3, 94**; 20-31
Lauds:	**66, 50**; 117, 62; **148-150**
Prime:	118: 1-4
Terce:	118: 5-7
Sext:	118: 8-10
None:	118: 11-13
Vespers:	109-112
Compline:	**4, 9, 133**

(The tabulation is based on John Chamberlin, *The Rule of St. Benedict: The Abingdon Copy* [Toronto, 1982], 82. For the names of the service hours I have followed English usage as reflected in Timothy Fry, *The Rule of Saint Benedict in English* [New York, 1998]).

The purpose of the *Opus Dei* and of a monk's existence was to praise God for the gift of life, and to that end the Psalms were ideally suited. Years of constant reiteration made Bede into a living Psalter, and his writings are filled with citations from and allusions to the Psalms.

Bede's *Abbreviated Psalter* is a direct outgrowth of his devotion to the *Opus Dei*. Crafted for personal prayer, meditation, and reflection, the booklet consists of extracts carefully chosen from each of the Psalms to represent their essence.

Benedicta Ward admirably summarizes Bede's focus, when she writes in *Bede and the Psalter* (Jarrow Lecture, 1991):

> [Bede] popularised [the use of the Psalms] by composing a new kind of prayer from them in his *Abbreviated Psalter*.... He selected verses from each Psalm which could be used as direct prayer or praise, as food for meditation, plea for mercy, protest, con-

trition, or adoration and exultation. Sometimes one verse alone was used, sometimes several. The verses were also selected so that a sense of the meaning of the Psalm as a whole was retained; it would be possible to recall the whole Psalm from these clues. . . . The text is both a compendium of the whole Psalter and a key to each Psalm, as well as a collection of phrases admirably suited to private and personal prayer (p. 10).

The text that Bede used for his *Abbreviated Psalter* is Jerome's Latin translation *iuxta Hebraeos* ("according to the Hebrews"). For the early church every verse in the Old Testament — including the Psalter — was understood as allegorically referring to the New. (For example, Psalm 1, which begins with the words "Blessed is the man who has not gone away in the counsel of the ungodly," was understood to refer to Jesus Christ.) In his translation, Jerome sought at times to make the reference to the New Testament explicit; this is especially obvious when, for the Hebrew word for "salvation," he substituted "Jesus": this the reader will see below in Psalms 50:14, 78:9, 84:5, and 149:4.

Another illustration of the allegorical interpretation of the Psalter may be found in verse 9 of No. 136, the great Psalm of compunction ("By the waters of Babylon..."). Verse 9 reads "Blessed is he who takes your children and dashes them against the stones." Everywhere else in his *Abbreviated Psalter* Bede used the text of the Psalms as the basis for his selection, but here alone — perhaps sensitive to the shock that a literal reading of the verse could induce — he substituted allegory: "Blessed is the man who fears the Lord." For his interpretation he may have drawn inspiration from St. Hilary, whose exposition of the verse in question reads: "Blessed ... is he who ... will drive

out and destroy each desire of his every passion ...
in accordance with the *fear* of God" (for the Latin see
Patrologia Latina 9 [Paris, 1844], 784B).

For the *Abbreviated Psalter* we lack Bede's autograph
and must rely instead on three Latin manuscripts written about a century after his death. Works copied by
hand are of course subject to scribal corruption, and
the *Abbreviated Psalter* is no exception, but by carefully
examining the evidence of the manuscripts we can
establish a text which for all practical purposes cor-
responds to what Bede intended.

In rendering Bede's *Abbreviated Psalter* into English,
I have used my critical edition of the Latin text:
Collectio Psalterii Bedae Venerabili adscripta, Bibliotheca
Scriptorum Graecorum et Romanorum Teubneriana
(K.G. Saur Verlag, Munich and Leipzig, 2001). My
translation makes no claim to originality but draws
freely from various versions of the complete Psalter.

I should point out that at times I have been guided by Cassiodorus's *Exposition of the Psalms*, a book well known to Bede. For example, in Psalm 1:1 Jerome writes *abiit*, literally "has gone away," which I keep in my translation (modern versions follow the Hebrew and write "walks" or the like); Cassiodorus tells us that *abiit* is to be understood as *recessit a praecepto Domini* ("has withdrawn from the precept of the Lord" — see *Corpus Christianorum Series Latina* 97 [Turnhout, 1958], 31.160). I have also consulted the translation that Benedicta Ward prints as an appendix to her Jarrow lecture; but despite her useful and insightful comments about the *Abbreviated Psalter*, the translation itself is based on a defective Latin text and does not in every instance correspond to what Bede selects. I should here note that, in abridging Jerome's version, Bede will often choose only part of a verse, without indicating what he omits. In this practice I have followed him; the reader will have to consult a complete Psalter to see how much is left out. The reader should also note that I have been guided by the critical edition of Jerome's complete text in R. Weber et al., *Biblia Sacra iuxta Vulgatam versionem*, ed. 4 (Stuttgart, 1994); hence for much of the book the numbers of the Psalms are one digit lower than those of the Masoretic text (on which most modern translations depend), and there are also occasionally minor discrepancies in the verse numbers.

GERALD M. BROWNE

March 2001

The *Abbreviated* PSALTER
of the *Venerable* BEDE

I

¹Blessed is the man who has not gone away in the counsel of the ungodly, and in the way of sinners has not stood, and in the seat of the scornful has not sat. ²But in the law of the Lord is his delight, and on his law he shall meditate day and night. ³And he shall be like a tree transplanted by the streams of waters, which shall give its fruit in its time, and its leaf shall not fall off; and everything that he does shall prosper.

2

[10]Now therefore, you kings, understand; be instructed, you judges of the earth. [11]Serve the Lord with fear, and exult in him with trembling. [12]Worship in purity, lest perchance he become angry, and you perish from the way.

3

[4]But you, Lord, are a shield around me, my glory and the lifter up of my head. [7]Arise, Lord; make me safe, my God.

4

[2]Have mercy on me, and hear my prayer.

5

[2]Hear my words, Lord; consider my murmuring, [3]my king and my God, [4]for I entreat you. [9]Lord, lead me in your righteousness on account of those who plot against me; make straight your way before my face.

6

²Lord, do not in your fury rebuke me, nor in your anger reproach me. ³Have mercy on me, Lord, for I am weak; heal me, Lord, for my bones are vexed, ⁴and my soul is vexed greatly; and you, Lord, how long? ⁵Return, Lord, rescue my soul; save me on account of your mercy.

7

²Lord my God, in you I have trusted; save me from all who persecute me, and deliver me, ³lest perchance he seize my soul like a lion and tear it, and there be none to come to the rescue.

8

²Lord our master, how great is your name in all the earth!

9

³I will be glad and rejoice in you; I will sing to your name, Most High. ³³⁽¹²⁾Arise, Lord God; lift up your hand; do not forget the poor.

10

[6]The Lord tries the righteous:

11

[2]save us, Lord.

12

[3]How long shall my enemy be exalted over me? [4]Turn, hear me, Lord my God. Illuminate my eyes, lest ever I sleep in death, [5]lest ever my enemy say: I have prevailed against him.

13

[7]Jacob shall exult, and Israel shall rejoice.

14

[4]But God glorifies those who fear the Lord.

15

[1]Guard me, God, for I have trusted in you, [2]saying to God: You are my Lord; it is not well with me without you.

er fortitudo me

nobis &redim

nus tuus dm ins

confitebuntur

&fortitudo a

ualidum; Re

atedo cantte c

16

¹Attend to my entreaty; give ear to my prayer. ⁵Support my goings on your paths, and my footsteps shall not slip. ⁶Incline your ear to me; hear my word. ⁷Make marvellous your mercy, savior of those who trust in you. ⁸Guard me like the pupil within the eye; in the shadow of your wings protect me. ¹⁵And I in righteousness will behold your face.

17

²I will love you, Lord, my strength.

18

[13]From my secret faults cleanse me; [14]from the presumptuous sins too deliver your servant. [15]Let the words of my mouth be pleasing, Lord, my strength and my redeemer.

19

[8]But we will remember the name of the Lord our God.

20

[14]Be exalted, Lord, in your strength; we will sing and praise your strengths.

21

[20]But you, Lord, do not be far; my strength, hasten to my help. [21]Rescue my soul from the sword; [22]save me from the mouth of the lion.

22

[6]And goodness and mercy follow me all the days of my life,

23

[5]and I will receive blessing from the Lord.

24

¹To you, Lord, I will lift up my soul. ⁴Show me your
ways, Lord; teach me your paths. ⁵Lead me in your
truth, and teach me, for you are God my savior. ⁷Do
not remember the sins of my youth, and my crimes.
In accordance with your mercy remember me. ¹¹On
account of your name pardon my iniquity, for it is
great. ¹⁶Look upon me and have mercy on me; ¹⁷from
my distresses bring me forth. ¹⁸Behold my humility
and my toil, and bear all my sins. ²⁰Guard my soul,
and deliver me.

25

⁸Lord, I have loved the habitation of your house. ⁹Do not take away my soul with the sinners; ¹¹redeem me and have mercy on me.

26

¹The Lord is my light and my salvation: whom shall I fear? ⁷Hear, Lord, my voice when I call upon you; have mercy on me and hear me. ⁹Do not hide your face from me; do not turn in fury from your servant. You have been my help: do not abandon me, and do not desert me, God my savior. ¹¹Show me, Lord, your way, and lead me in the right path on account of those who plot against me. ¹²Do not deliver me, Lord, to the will of those who afflict me. ¹³And I believe that I shall see the goodness of the Lord in the land of the living.

27

²Hear, Lord, my entreaty, when I cry to you. ³Do not deliver me with the ungodly and with those who work iniquity. ⁷The Lord is my strength and my shield.

28

²Adore the Lord in holy majesty.

29

¹¹Hear, Lord, and have mercy on me. Lord, be my helper, ¹³so that honor may praise you and not be silent. Lord my God, forever will I glorify you.

30

[2]In you, Lord, I have trusted; let me not be put to confusion forever: in your righteousness save me. [3]Incline your ear to me; quickly deliver me. [4]Because you are my rock and my defense, [6]in your hand I will place my spirit. [16]In your hand are my times. Deliver me from the hand of my enemies and those who persecute me. [17]Show your face to your servant; save me in your mercy.

31

[1]Blessed is he whose iniquity is forgiven, and whose sin is covered. [5]My sin I make known to you, and my iniquity I do not cover. [7]You are my protection; from the enemy you will guard me.

ea quare. pro

nenos propter

saeculum inae

insaeculum e

auxilium int

ex magnus

cante re̅ inr̅o

32

[18]Behold, the eyes of the Lord are upon those who fear him, and who expect his mercy. [22]Let your mercy, Lord, be upon us, according as we have expected you.

33

[2]I will bless the Lord at all times; his praise is always in my mouth. [4]Magnify the Lord with me, and let us exalt his name together. [5]I sought the Lord, and he heard me; and from all my distresses he delivered me. [9]Taste and see that the Lord is good; blessed is the man who trusts in him. [10]Fear the Lord, you his saints, for there is no lack for those who fear him. [11]And for those who seek the Lord no good thing shall be

wanting. ²¹The Lord guards all their bones; none of them shall be broken. ²³The Lord shall redeem the souls of his servants.

34

¹Judge, Lord, my adversaries; fight against those who fight me. ²Take shield and spear, and arise for my help. ³Say to my soul: I am your salvation. ⁹And my soul shall exult in the Lord, and it shall rejoice in its salvation. ¹⁸I will praise you in the great congregation, ²⁸and my tongue shall meditate on your righteousness, on your praise for the whole day.

35

^{6}Lord, in heaven is your mercy. ^{8}How precious is your mercy, Lord, ^{10}for with you is the fountain of life, and in your light we shall see light. ^{11}Bring your mercy to those who know you, and your righteousness to the upright in heart. ^{12}Let not the foot of pride come against me, and let not the hand of the ungodly disturb me.

36

^{25}I was a boy, and indeed I have become old; and I have not seen the righteous forsaken, ^{28}for the Lord loves judgment, and he shall not forsake his saints; forever they are guarded, ^{40}and the Lord shall help them.

37

[2]Lord, do not in your anger rebuke me, nor in your fury reproach me. [16]For you, Lord, I was expecting; you will hear, Lord my God. [21]Because I followed the good, [22]do not forsake me. Lord my God, do not be far from me; [23]hasten to my help, Lord, God of my salvation.

38

[8]You are my expectation: [9]from all my iniquities deliver me. Do not make me a reproach for the fool; [11]take your scourges from me.

39

[2]Expectantly I expected the Lord, and he inclined to me, [3]and he heard my cry: [14]Lord, hasten to help me. [17]Let those who seek you be glad and rejoice in you. [18]You are my help and my salvation: my God, do not delay.

40

[5]I said: Lord, have mercy on me; heal my soul, for I have sinned against you. [11]And you, Lord, have mercy on me.

4I

[2]Like a garden prepared for the irrigation of waters, so my soul is prepared for you, God.

42

[1]Judge me, God, and defend my cause against an unholy nation; from a man deceitful and unjust save me. [2]For you are my strength: why have you cast me away?

43

[26]Arise, help us, and redeem us on account of your mercy.

44

[7]Your throne, God, is forever and ever. [18]Therefore the peoples shall praise you forever and ever.

45

[2]Our God, you are found to be hope and strength, a mighty help in tribulations.

46

[3]He is the great king over all the earth. [7]Sing to God, sing; sing to our king, sing.

ecisti me surg
misericordia
ernum; pr
ina &ernum;
bulationibu
super omnem
cante; Quia

47

[15]For it is he who is God, our God forever and ever; it is he who will be our leader in death.

48

[16]But God shall redeem my soul from the hand of hell, when he receives me.

49

[1]The mighty God, the Lord, said: [8]Not on account of your sacrifices will I rebuke you, and your burnt offerings are before me always. [9]I will not take a calf from your house, nor goats from the folds. [10]For mine are all the animals of the forests. [11]I know all the birds

of the mountains, and all the beasts of the field are with me. [12]If I am hungry, I will not tell you; for mine is the earth and its fulness. [14]Offer praise to God, and pay your vows to the Most High. [15]And call upon me in the day of tribulation: I will deliver you, and you shall glorify me. [23]He who offers praise glorifies me, and as for him who walks modestly, I will show him my salvation.

50

[3]Have mercy on me, God, in accordance with your great mercy. According to the multitude of your compassions blot out my iniquities. [4]Wash me thoroughly from my iniquity, and from my sin cleanse me, [5]for I know my iniquities, and my sin is before me always. [6]Against you alone I have sinned, and I have done evil before you. [11]Hide your face from my sins, and all my iniquities

blot out. [12]Create for me a clean heart, God, and a steadfast spirit renew in my inner parts. [13]Do not cast me away from your face, and do not take your holy spirit from me. [14]Restore to me the joy of your Jesus, and with powerful spirit strengthen me. [16]Deliver me from bloody deeds, God, God of my salvation; my tongue shall praise your righteousness. [17]Lord, you shall open my lips, and my mouth shall declare your praise. [19]The sacrifice of God is a troubled spirit; a heart contrite and brought low God shall not despise.

51

[3]The mercy of God is for the whole day. [10]I, like a green olive tree in the house of God, have trusted in the mercy of God forever.

52

[7]Jacob shall exult, and Israel shall rejoice.

53

[3]God, in your name save me, and in your strength avenge me. [4]God, hear my prayer; give ear to the words of my mouth.

54

[2]Hear, God, my prayer, and do not despise my entreaty; [3]attend to me and hear me. [24]And I have faith in you.

55

⁴In whatever day I am terrified, I will trust in you. ⁵I will not fear what flesh may do to me; ¹⁰this I know, that you are my God.

56

²Have mercy on me, God; have mercy on me, for my soul has trusted in you. In the shadow of your wings I will trust, until the treachery passes away. ³I will call upon God the Most High, God my avenger. ⁴He shall send from heaven, and he shall save me.

57

¹²Truly there is a God who judges on the earth.

58

²Rescue me from my enemies, my God, and from those who oppose me protect me. ¹⁰I will keep for you my strength, for you are God, my deliverer; ¹¹the mercy of my God shall go before me. ¹⁷Because you have become my strength, and refuge in the day of my tribulation, ¹⁸to you I will sing, for God is my helper, my strength; God is my mercy.

59

¹³Give us help in affliction, for vain is the salvation from man. ¹⁴Through God we will act valiantly, and it is he who shall trample upon those who afflict us.

60

²Hear, God, my praise; attend to my prayer. ³From the end of the earth I will cry to you, when my heart is sad. When a strong man rises up against me, you shall be my teacher. ⁴You have been my hope, a tower most secure against the face of the enemy. ⁵I will dwell in your tabernacle forever; I will trust in the protection of your wings. ⁶For you, God, have heard my prayer; you have given an inheritance to those who fear your name. ⁸Mercy and truth shall preserve him.

61

⁶For from him is my expectation. ⁷It is he who is my strength and my salvation, my protector: I will not fear.

& auxiliare

ntuam ; thro

pter eapopuli

ड़ो ñnoster sper

inuentuser

ettam ; Can

psee dñnoster

62

²God, you are my strength; at dawn I will rise to you.
My soul has thirsted for you, my flesh has longed
for you. ³Thus in the sanctuary I have appeared to
you, so that I may see your strength and your glory.
⁴Your mercy is better than life; my lips shall praise you.
⁵Thus I will bless you in my life; in your name I will lift
up my hands. ⁸Because you have been my help, in the
shadow of your wings I will sing praises.

63

²Hear, God, my voice when I speak; from fear of the
enemy preserve my life.

64

[6]Hear us, God our savior.

65

[4]Let all the earth adore you, and it shall sing to you, it shall sing to your name. [8]Bless, you peoples, our God, and make heard the voice of his praise; [9]he ordained our soul for life. [20]Blessed be the Lord, who has not taken away my prayer and his mercy from me.

66

[2]May God have mercy on us and bless us; may he make his face shine upon us. [7]May God, our God, bless us; [8]may God bless us.

67

²Let God arise, and let his enemies be scattered; and let those who hate him flee from his face. ⁴But let the just rejoice; let them exult in the presence of God, and let them be glad in joy.

68

¹⁷Hear me, Lord, for your mercy is good; in accordance with the multitude of your compassions look upon me. ¹⁸And do not hide your face from your servant; because I am afflicted, hear me quickly. ¹⁹Come near to my soul and redeem it; on account of my enemies deliver me: ³⁰your salvation, God, has protected me.

69

²God, hasten to deliver me; Lord, hasten to help me.
⁵Let all who seek you be glad and rejoice in you. ⁶And
I am needy and poor; God, hasten for me. You are my
help and my savior: Lord, do not delay.

70

¹In you, Lord, I have trusted; let me not be put to
confusion forever: ²in your righteousness rescue me
and deliver me. Incline your ear to me, and save me.
⁴My God, save me from the hand of the ungodly, from
the hand of the unjust and harmful, ⁵for you are my
hope, Lord. ¹²God, do not be far from me; my God,
hasten to my help.

71

[17]Your name shall be forever; beyond the sun your name shall endure.

72

[28]And for me it is good to draw near to God; I have placed my hope in the Lord God.

73

[12]And God is my king from the beginning. [19]Do not deliver to the beasts the soul instructed in your law; do not forget the life of your poor forever.

74

[10]And I will declare forever; I will sing to the God of Jacob,

75

[10]when God arises to judge, to make safe all the meek of the earth.

76

[2]With my voice I cried to the Lord, with my voice to God, and he heard me. [3]In the day of my tribulation I sought God.

77

[38]But it is he who, being merciful, shall pardon iniquity, and he shall not destroy it.

78

[8]Do not remember our old iniquities; let your mercies quickly come to us, for we are very weak. [9]Help us, God our Jesus, on account of the glory of your name, and deliver us and pardon our sins on account of your name.

79

[3]Arouse your strength, and come to make us safe. [8]God of hosts, turn us, and show your face, and we shall be safe.

insaeculum &

Uerum tamen

ni cum adsump

propter uicti

tua cotam m

uitulum nequ

nimalia filu

stas agrimec

80

[2]Praise God our strength.

81

[3]Judge for the poor and the orphan; for the needy and indigent act justly. [4]Save the indigent and poor; deliver him from the hand of the ungodly.

82

[2]God, do not be silent, do not be quiet, and do not be still, God. [19]And let them know that your name is the Lord; you alone are High over all the earth.

83

⁹Lord God of hosts, hear my prayer. ¹³Lord of hosts, blessed is the man who trusts in you.

84

⁵Turn us, God our Jesus, and relax your anger against us. ⁶Do not be angry with us forever. ⁸Show us, Lord, your mercy, and your salvation give to us.

85

¹Incline, Lord, your ear; hear me, for I am needy and poor. ³Have mercy on me, Lord, for to you I will cry for the whole day; ⁴make joyful the soul of your ser-

vant, for to you I lift up my soul. [5]For you, Lord, are good and forgiving, and abounding in mercy for all who call upon you. [6]Hear, Lord, my prayer, and listen to the voice of my entreaties. [7]In the day of my tribulation I will call upon you, for you will hear me. [11]Teach me, Lord, your way, that I may walk in your truth. Make single my heart, that it may fear your name. [12]I will praise you, Lord my God, with my whole heart, and I will glorify your name forever. [15]And you, Lord God, are merciful and loving. [16]Look upon me and have mercy on me; give your strength to your servant, and save the son of your handmaiden. [17]Make with me a sign in goodness, and let those who hate me see and be put to confusion, because you, Lord, have helped me, and you have consoled me.

86

[7]And they shall sing as in choirs: All my springs are in you.

87

[3]Let my prayer come before you; incline your ear to my praise. [14]And I have cried to you, Lord, and in the morning my prayer shall come before you.

88

[6]The heavens shall praise your wonders, Lord; [15]mercy and truth shall go before your face.

89

[16]Let your work appear before your servants, and your glory to their sons. [17]And let the majesty of the Lord our God be upon us, and establish the work of our hands.

90

[9]For you, Lord, are my hope,

91

[5]for you, Lord, have made me joyful through your work.

92

[5]Your testimonies have become very trustworthy;

93

[18]your mercy, Lord, has supported me.

94

[6]Come, let us adore and bow down; let us bend our knees before the face of the Lord our creator, [7]for it is he who is the Lord our God.

95

[6]Glory and majesty are before his face.

96

[10]You who love the Lord, hate evil: he guards the souls of his saints; from the hand of the ungodly he shall rescue them.

nperp&uum

df redim& ar

sritme; For

as tuas; arq

sunt semper;

degregibus

rum scio omn

ameft; Siesu

97

[3]He has remembered his mercy:

98

[5]exalt the Lord our God.

99

[2]Serve the Lord in joy; come before him in praise.

[3]Know that it is the Lord who is God; it is he who

made us, and we are his.

100

[1]Of mercy and judgment I will sing to you, Lord; I will sing psalms, [2]and I will be instructed in the perfect way as to when you will come to me.

101

[2]Lord, hear my prayer, and let my cry come to you. [3]Do not hide your face from me; in the day of my tribulation incline your ear to me. In whatever day I call upon you, quickly hear me.

102

[1]Bless the Lord, my soul, and all my inner parts his holy name. [2]Bless the Lord, my soul, and do not forget all his recompenses; [3]he pardons all your iniquities, and he heals all your weaknesses; [4]he shall redeem your life from corruption, and he crowns you with mercy and compassions.

103

[1]Bless the Lord, my soul. Lord my God, you are greatly magnified. With glory and majesty you are clothed. [31]Let the glory of the Lord be forever; the Lord shall rejoice in his works.

104

⁴Seek the Lord and his power; seek his face forever.
⁵Remember the wonders that he has done.

105

³Blessed are those who keep judgment, and who do righteousness at all times. ⁴⁷Save us, Lord our God, that we may praise your holy name and sing, as we glorify you: ⁴⁸Blessed be the Lord God of Israel.

106

¹Praise the Lord, for he is good, for his mercy is forever. ⁸Let the Lord be praised for his mercies, and his wonders for the sons of men, ⁹for he has satisfied the empty soul, and the hungry soul he has filled with good things.

107

¹³Give us help in affliction, for vain is the salvation from man. ¹⁴Through God we will be strong, and it is he who shall trample upon our enemies.

108

²¹And you, Lord, deal with me on account of your name, since your mercy is good. Deliver me, ²²since I am needy and poor. ²⁶Help me, Lord my God; save me in accordance with your mercy.

109

²Rule in the midst of your enemies.

110

¹I will praise the Lord with my whole heart. ³Glory and majesty are his work; ⁷the work of his hands are truth and judgment.

III

[1]Blessed is the man who fears the Lord; in his commandments he shall delight greatly. [7]The righteous shall be in everlasting remembrance; of evil report he shall not be afraid.

112

[2]Blessed be the name of the Lord from now and forever.

113

[9(1)]Not to us, Lord, not to us, but to your name give glory, [10(2)]on account of your mercy and your truth.

...pserit luxn...

...umam meam...

...tur d̄s d̄n̄s loc...

...quamte &hol...

Nonaccipiar...

...hirchos · Me...

...es auesmonti...

...iero nondica...

114

[4]I beseech you, Lord; save my soul.

115

[13]And I will call upon the name of the Lord; [15]glorious in the sight of the Lord is the death of his saints,

116

[2]and the truth of the Lord is forever.

117

⁶You are the Lord my God: I will not fear what man may do to me. ⁷The Lord is my helper, and I will despise those who hate me. ⁸It is better to hope in the Lord than to hope in man. ⁹It is better to hope in the Lord than to hope in princes. ²¹I will praise you, Lord, for you have heard me, and you have become my salvation.

118

⁷I will praise you, Lord, in uprightness of heart, when I learn the judgments of your righteousness. ¹⁰Do not make me wander from your commandments. ¹⁸Unveil my eyes, and I will see the wonders in your law. ²⁹Remove the way of falsehood from me, and give

me your law. [36]Incline my heart to your testimonies, and not to avarice. [41]And let your mercies come upon me, Lord, and your salvation according to your word. [50]This is my consolation in my affliction, that your word has given me life. [64]The earth is full of your mercy: teach me your precepts. [67]Before I heard I was ignorant. [68]You are good and beneficent: teach me your precepts. [76]Let, I beseech, your mercy be for my consolation, according as you spoke to your servant. [88]In accordance with your mercy give me life, and I will keep the testimony of your mouth. [92]Except that your law had been my meditation, perchance I would have perished in my affliction. [103]How sweet to my throat is your word, more than honey to my mouth! [108]Let the freewill offerings of my mouth be pleasing to you, Lord, and in accordance with your judgments teach me. [116]Strengthen me in accordance with your word, and I will live; [117]help me, and I will be safe.

[124]Deal with your servant according to your mercy, and teach me your precepts. [132]Look upon me, and have mercy on me, [135]and teach me your precepts. [137]Righteous are you, Lord, and upright is your judgment.

[149]Hear my voice according to your mercy, Lord; in accordance with your judgment give me life. [153]See my affliction and rescue me; [159]according to your mercy give me life. [165]Great peace is for those who love your law, and in them there is no stumbling block. [169]Let my praise come before you, Lord; in accordance with your word teach me. [170]Let my entreaty come before your face; in accordance with your word deliver me.

119

[2]Lord, deliver my soul from the lip of falsehood, from the deceitful tongue.

120

[1]I have lifted up my eyes to the mountains, whence help is to come for me.

121

[6]Let it be well for those who love you.

122

³Have mercy on us, Lord, have mercy on us.

123

⁸Our help is in the name of the Lord, who made heaven and earth.

124

⁴Benefit, Lord, the good and upright in heart.

125

⁴Change, Lord, our captivity, like a stream in the south.

126

[1]Unless the Lord guards the city, he who guards it watches in vain.

127

[1]Blessed is everyone who fears the Lord, who walks in his ways.

128

[8]The blessing of the Lord be upon us.

oster inmontæ
demanu infer
utus est non
o causta mata
n dedomo tua
sunt enim om
um & uniuer
mabi meusē

129

[2]Lord, hear my voice; let your ears become attentive to the voice of my entreaty.

130

[1]Lord, my heart is not exalted, nor are my eyes lifted up.

131

[14]This is my rest forever,

132

³for there the Lord has commanded blessing and life forever.

133

¹You who stand in the house of the Lord,

134

³glorify the Lord, for the Lord is good.

135

²⁶Praise the God of heaven, for his mercy is forever.

136

[9]Blessed is the man who fears the Lord.

137

[1]I will praise you, Lord, with my whole heart. [8]Lord, your mercy is forever; do not forsake the works of your hands.

138

[8]If I ascend to heaven, you are there; if I lie in hell, you are present.

139

²Rescue me, Lord, from the evil man; from unjust men save me.

140

¹Hear my voice, as I cry to you. ²Let my prayer be directed like incense in your presence. ³Put a guard, Lord, on my mouth; keep the poverty of my lips.

141

⁸Bring my soul out of prison, that it may praise your name.

142

¹Lord, hear my prayer; hear me in your righteousness. ²And do not come to make judgment with your servant, for no one living shall be justified in your presence. ⁸Make me hear your mercy in the morning, for in you I trust. Make known to me the way in which I walk, for to you I will lift up my soul. ⁹Deliver me from my enemies, Lord: by you I am protected. ¹⁰Teach me to do your will, for you are my God. Your good spirit shall lead me in the upright land; ¹¹on account of your name, Lord, you will give me life in your righteousness. ¹²For I am your servant.

143

[1]Blessed be my mighty Lord, [2]my mercy and my strength, my helper and my savior.

144

[2]Every day I will bless you, and I will praise your name forever and ever. [21]My mouth shall speak the praise of the Lord, and all flesh shall bless his holy name forever and ever.

145

²Praise the Lord, my soul; I will praise the Lord in my life, I will sing to my God as long as I am.

146

¹Praise the Lord, for it is good. ¹¹The Lord takes pleasure in those who fear him, and who expect his mercy.

147

¹⁸He shall send his word, and he shall destroy them.

enim orbis ter

&redde altissi

tionis· liberab

fessionem glo

damei salutar

magnam mis

miserationum

labame abomn

148

¹Praise the Lord from the heavens; praise him in the heights. ²Praise him, all you his angels; praise him, all you his hosts. ³Praise him, sun and moon; praise him, all you stars of light. ⁴Praise him, you heavens of heavens, and let the waters which are above the heavens ⁵praise the name of the Lord, for it is he who commanded, and they were created. ¹¹Praise the Lord, you kings of the earth and all you peoples, you princes and all you judges of the earth. ¹²Let young men and maidens, old men with boys, praise the name of the Lord, ¹³for his name alone is lofty; ¹⁴his glory is in heaven and on earth. And he has exalted the horn of his people; praise is amongst all his saints.

149

¹Sing to the Lord a new song; his praise is in the congregation of saints. ⁴He shall exalt the meek through Jesus. ⁵The saints shall exult in glory; they shall sing praises in their beds. ⁶The exultations of God are in their throat.

150

⁶Let everything that breathes praise the Lord.